The 7 Power Keys to Positive Thinking

How to Be a Happy Person?

Darcy Davis

Let's Start to Think About Your Better Way! A Positive Journal and Book Help You Writing Prompts and Reflections for Living in the Present Moment!

If You Begin To Manage Your Thoughts,
You Will Be The Master Of Your Own Life.
Change a Life for The Better!

TABLE OF CONTENTS

INTRODUCTION 5

KEY 1: LIVING YOUR OWN LIFE.............................7

KEY 2: UNDERSTANDING THE QUALITIES OF THOSE WHO ARE POSITIVE.......................................17

KEY 3: REALIZING THAT NOTHING WILL CHANGE UNTIL YOU CHANGE YOUR THOUGHTS...29

KEY 4: CHANGING YOUR MINDSET TO POSITIVE THINKING 39

KEY 5: LEARNING TO ACCEPT YOURSELF.......49

KEY 6: REALIZING MISTAKES ARE JUST A SIMULATOR TO MAKE YOU STRONGER 57

KEY 7: THE POWER OF LOVE AND GRATITUDE 66

CONCLUSION 72

INTRODUCTION

Positive thoughts are powerful, and they can drastically change your life. Having positive thoughts can give you a better understanding of yourself and the motivation to be successful.

If there is anything you want to change, whether it is yourself, your life, or the world around you, you can do so with positive thoughts. You should work to achieve positivity because it goes a long way.

Think about it: will you really achieve your dreams if you're walking around thinking you can't do something? Chances are, you will probably falter.

Positivity plays a major role, and thoughts are more powerful than you think.

In this book, I'll give you 7 keys in order to change your life and they all relate to the power of positivity. These seven positive keys can help you to become better than you've ever been.

If you've ever felt stumped in life, or if you feel like you need motivation to be happier, then look no further. With each of these keys, you'll get a reason why these keys are

important, and how you can apply them with some helpful exercises to help you hone these skills.

Everyone can change his or her life for the better. You'd be surprised at the difference that this mindset makes, and also what you can achieve with this approach. Instead of worrying so much about the past, you can learn to let go, move on from the problems of the past, and learn to live the best life you possibly can!

Once you finish reading all 7 of the keys here, you'll be able to utilize positivity in your life, whether it is trying to score a job, finding a compatible life partner, or making a profound difference as far as spiritual, environmental, or societal aims.

While it may seem like you're just one person, you really aren't, since you play a major role in the collective future you want to create.

KEY 1:

LIVING YOUR OWN LIFE

Living your own life might be something you think you're already doing, but chances are it's not to its fullest potential.

Do you tend to follow the trends instead of branching out and doing your own thing? Have you tried to change yourself for other people?

If the answer is yes to at least one of these questions, then it's time to learn how to live your own life and not rely on other people.

The first step is learning to accept yourself, which includes not just physical features and flaws, but also key emotional and mental aspects of yourself. You may be ashamed of the fact that you have some "flaw" but learning to accept it will deeply impact your life.

If you don't learn how to accept yourself, you're going to have a problem. That's because everything you do from here on out, if you're not being yourself, will feel fake, disingenuous, and disappointed.

In fact, we often rely on societal aspects to be happy, such as fashion, as if you have the latest iPhone or newest computer model, then you're successful.

But does this comparative approach really gauge one's success?

No, it doesn't. Because last time I checked, an iPhone is a machine, and not something personal. The pursuit of material objects is often an obsession in our society, to the point where we will sacrifice a part of ourselves for these material objects.

For example, let's say someone goes into a business or field they absolutely hate but does it merely for the money. Sure, one is making a lot, but is the person truly happy? The chances are high, that she's not. Instead, dream is typically imposed by an external force, such as a family member or even one's parents.

The pursuit of material goods and means is an obsession for many, and for some, they become almost zombies, trying to obtain these objects. But these material goods don't measure success; rather, your own personal happiness is your ultimate success. Happiness in what you do is true success, remember that!

Everyone has his or her own means for success, a personal definition of what "success" is. You need to look into yourself, and see what you believe to be true success. It may not even be a monetary goal. It can be "raising a beautiful family" or "traveling the world." Determine what your own success is, and from there, you can pursue the path of living your own life happily and authentically!

Those who are successful don't deal with the affairs of others or let them control their lives. Instead, they understand that others have their own measure of "success," and they live up to those expectations. Understanding that you have your own version of success is super important.

TIME TO THINK AND WRITE

Who are you? What do you want to be?

What do you want to do?

What do you want to do now?
What do you realize about yourself?

Everyone's Vision of Success is Different

If you're wondering whether your vision of success is correct or not, the answer is up to you. Many of us have different levels of success, so we gauge our success based on others at times. That shouldn't be done though.

Everyone has his or her own battles to fight, his or her own issues to overcome. If you continue to gauge your success on the affairs of others, you're only going to make yourself upset.

The biggest concept to realize is that everyone does have different levels of success, and everyone views success in diverse ways. Even between husband and wife, success can be unique, and that's something people tend to forget. Some women don't realize that their own happiness is a little different from what their partners might deem as success. For example, let's say that you have a goal of wanting to go back to college and be successful.

Some people don't view that as success. Some see college as a waste of time and money, not something worth investing in. and that's fine, not everyone is the same.

If you go into life realizing that everyone is different, and that you shouldn't compare yourself to others so much, it can save you a lot of headaches in the future.

That is something you need to take from this book: stop comparing your success to other people. The key to success, is actually to stop looking so much at others' achievements but instead look at your own success to compare personal successes of the past to the future accomplishments. That's what you need to realize, and what you have to take from this guide.

So what does that mean for you? Well, it should indicate that the best way to generate your own personal success isn't through just looking through the lens of others, but instead, focusing on yourself.

Compare yourself to who you were before, not to anyone else, and from there, you'll be able to understand your potential. When comparing your life, stop equating it to other people. Don't worry so much about what Joe Schmo is doing, but instead look at the reality of life, what you can change for yourself, and praise how far you've come.

By looking at life, seeing how far you've come, and where you plan on going, you'll be successful. You'll be able to generate more success from this strategic than you've ever imagined!

Stop judging yourself, and start looking at what will make you happy!

TIME TO THINK AND WRITE

What is your success?

What needs to be done to succeed?

How to Understand Your Own Success

The best way to understand your own success is simple. Sit down, and brainstorm what your ideal levels of success would be. Would it involve having a big home, two kids, a successful job, and a stable income? Or would it be to

travel the world and see as many cultures as possible? Whatever it might be, write it down vividly.

From here, determine if you're truly living up to this potential or working towards it. If not, why is that?

Write down which factors are holding your back, and why you may not be living your ideal life.

At that point, write down steps you can take in order to achieve the life that you desire.

At this point, understand that your own success is critical to living the best life that you can. Do something that contributes to your own success in life, and don't just follow in others' footsteps.

It is important that you create the best life that you feel is right for you.

Don't make it based off what others have. Don't measure your success based on other people's work and happiness. Instead, make your own life, do what is right for you, and you'll be even happier!

TIME TO THINK AND WRITE

Write down which factors are holding your back, and why you may not be living your ideal life.

KEY 2: UNDERSTANDING THE QUALITIES OF THOSE WHO ARE POSITIVE

Do you ever just marvel at those people who are always positive? How does that even work? How can you achieve a more positive outlook?

Well, it involves a few aspects that you'll want to figure out for yourself, and different qualities that can ultimately change your life. Here, I'll discuss a few of the qualities that positive people have and how discuss how you can learn to be more positive.

Energy and Positivity!

Positive people tend to have quality energy. What does that mean?

Have you ever been around someone that just makes you feel really good? I love those types of people.

They're great at getting everyone in a good mood, tend to be happy, and encourage others to spend lots of time with them. These are good examples of positive people.

Positive people radiate that energy that makes you go "wow, I feel so much better than before" and they can revitalize you.

They usually are the types of people that don't bore you or stress you out, that feel great to be around, and you don't feel bored or drained being around them. It's quite nice, and when you find these people, you typically leave conversations feeling refreshed and happy.

Usually, negative people to the opposite: they exude toxic energy that is hard to deal with and are frustrating to be near. If you have people that you always want to get away from, they are likely not as positive as you think.

Energies are natural parts of a person. We all have certain kind of energy, but it's often something we don't even realize.

The best way to gauge your type of energy is to look at the way others treat you. Do they look at you with appreciation, like being around you, and want to spend time with you? If the answer to that is yes, then you've probably got positive energy. This trait is a major characteristic of people, and something many take for granted.

TIME TO THINK

Energy is a big part, and if you're wondering whether someone is positive or a good influence, think about the energy they exhibit, how you feel when you spend time with them, and how you feel when you're done. These questions will facilitate your answer!

Look at Their Lives

Positive people are typically really happy, but they aren't just acting like that for fun: they really do have good lives. Usually, they have strong mental and physical health, in that they aren't getting sick all the time, and they usually are pretty strong.

They also tend to be successful at work, perform jobs that they love, and feel good about. If they hate their job and are always complaining about it, chances are they probably aren't as positive as you presume.

Their families tend to be happy, too. Now, that doesn't mean they have children in each instance. They can be successful and be childfree. Usually though, they have a tight-knit family and have a successful, enjoyable and happy family life.. If they don't have a family, they usually have strong relationships with their friends, or a relationship that allows them to really be happy. Remember, family doesn't always need to be blood-related, so look at their peers, too.

Life doesn't have to be perfect, but you can look at these people and see what they're doing. Are they actively working towards a goal, or are they just floundering around, not doing anything? Do they tend to just sleep a lot and never accomplish anything in life? Or are they actively working towards a bright and interesting future? Sometimes, even just seeing how they are in life, or if they're going towards any goals, can express a lot about someone.

Happiness is often a big part of a positive person. While life isn't always sunshine and rainbows, their lives are generally happy and full of a purpose, which in turn allows them to have a better outlook on life.

TIME TO THINK

What happiness is yours?

At what moments in life are you happy?

The Importance of a Desire to Live

One of the biggest characteristics of a positive person is the desire to live. Life might not always be easy, but usually, if you have a reason for sticking around, you'll find ways to make life happier.

Typically, even on the worst of days, those who want to live will look at life with a positive, rather than a negative outlook. People who care about their well-being will want to live, and that's a huge part of being a positive person.

For example, have you ever felt your purposes all align, and you feel that spark of life? You may realize that "hey, I'm moving towards a goal, I can do this!" That desire to live can help you propel forward so that you can continue on.

In contrast, if you feel like you're just floundering around, not doing anything, then you're not going to be as happy. You tend to feel more lost than on-purpose.

It doesn't mean always being happy, but you need to have a reason to stick around, and that reason can help you even on the roughest of days.

I know it's hard sometimes, but one major part of success is learning how to be a more positive person, and learning to harness the negative energy in order to not let it affect you. Sometimes, purpose alone can make you a happier and more successful person.

Purposes are important. If you have a purpose, you'll feel more inspired. You will feel better, and even if that purpose is something trivial, it does make a major difference. If you want to be successful, then you need to have a reason for persevering.

This mindset goes for anything, not just getting up in the morning or existing. A business is only as successful as long as it has a purpose, and a person is as successful as long as he or she has a purpose. Without one, life kind of turns into this boring chore, and you kind of end up hating it. A purposeless life tends to create a bit of a burden, not just on yourself but others, too.

If you have a purpose, then you'll have a reason for getting up in the morning. That purpose could be to have another killer day at work, or to wake up and see your lovely spouse. Whatever it may be, one of the important characteristics of a positive person is having a reason for enduring.

TIME TO THINK AND WRITE

THE 7 GOAL IDEAS

What you must do to achieve your goals?

How You can be a more Positive Person

So how can you be a more positive person? Well, it's all up to you. You need to determine which areas of life you're not being as positive in and work towards a solution.

We recommend the following:

- Sit down and look at every area of your life to reflect they're doing. Be honest with the evaluation.

- If there are areas that you're not doing well in, be honest and confirm them.

- Next, look at different ways you can change that part of your life, so the outlook is better, whether it be building a healthier relationship with your partner, working towards a job you enjoy, or even just thinking about the good in people.

- From here, formulate a plan and really be honest about what you need to do. Make a timetable to determine how long it will take to accomplish each step.

- Every single day you should wake up, look at this plan. Next, begin to work on each of these targets. Whether it involves distributing job applications, going out on dates or with friends, or even just not reading social media as much, doing each of these tasks every day in increments will change you in a positive manner!

- If you need to talk to someone, tell another about your plan to be a better person and goal to be more positive. They'll likely support you, and it will help you push forward, no matter what happens next.

Just by doing this social connection, you'll be able to form a healthier relationship with yourself. Take the actions listed t in the first key as well regarding your own personal success. Work towards that success. Many who are positive tend to be more goal-oriented, so you'll want to ensure that each time you do look at the list, you're working towards success.

This goal focus can be hard, especially if you have doubts about ever being positive. Maybe you've lived a life that's been full of ups and downs, with more downs than ups happening as of late? While it can be stressful, you should strive to be more positive. This attribute alone will bring you additional success. Take that negativity, those hardships and faltering situations, and don't let them control you. Instead learn to better yourself and become the most positive person you can be. There is no magic potion to change your outlook, so you just need to be more positive!

One of the keys to happiness and success in life is positivity. Very few get things done with a negative mindset. While it can be hard to truly follow this one, you should every day look for a positive aspect of yourself, your life, and others, and from there, focus on this approach. By working to have an outlook on your life and mastering this, you'll realize being successful is possible. There is a reason why this is one of the seven keys to success.

Positivity, even just a little bit, will go a long way. You just have to shift your mindset, which we will discuss in the next chapter.

TIME TO THINK AND WRITE

Please write your positive expression that will motivate you!

Let's Start to Think About Your Better Way!

KEY 3:
REALIZING THAT NOTHING WILL CHANGE UNTIL YOU CHANGE YOUR THOUGHTS

This one is a bit harder. But, unfortunately we are all responsible for our own destinies. What does that mean for you? Well, it reiterates that if you want to change something in your life, no matter how big or how small, you've got to change your mindset. Many people focus on the doom and gloom of life, and unfortunately, this common issue plagues many of us. If our lives aren't the way that we want them to be, sometimes changing your mindset is harder than you think. But let's be real, you won't be able to accomplish anything with a mindset that's negative, right? Let's take for example the desire to have a new job. Maybe you've had the mindset that "this job is the best one I'll get, and I'll never be able to get anything better." That mindset is going to stop you from getting a new job.

You'll try to complete application after application, but you'll just get denied each time.

That stinks, right?

Well, what about if you have the mindset of "I'll never get a boyfriend", "No one will love me," and other negative vibes, if you want a relationship. If you are trying super hard to find someone going on date after date, but it's just not working, maybe it might be you, or rather your thought process.

Thoughts have immense power. You know the phrase, "If you believe it, you can achieve it," right? That applies to your thoughts and desires. If you do believe you can get something, or you want to change your life, you've first got to look at the thought process that you're using.

Think about some of the different aspects of life that you want to improve. Maybe you want a bigger house, but you're afraid of the down payments, or perhaps you want to get married to your partner, but you fear commitment. All of these beliefs can hold you back, and the reality is that your thought processes can hold you back more than you think.

One important factor you should consider when working towards a successful and happier life, is to look at the different aspects YOU want to improve and change your mindset.

The law of attraction applies to this premise, too. Have you ever heard of that? Essentially, it means that you'll attract what you put out into the world. If you're positive and you extend a positive thought, you'll get that. In the same vein, if you're negative, you're going to attract that negativity like flies to honey.

The first step to understand and accept is that nothing will change until you decide to change it. You won't be able to progress with your goals, dreams, or whatever it might be until your thoughts are aligned with the goals you have.

What that means is, if you don't really want it, and you're not trying to exude positive energy, you can say goodbye to changing your life. Positive energy works wonders with this tenet of logic, and you need to make the decision to change.

Having the desire to change goes with anything. Let's take for example an alcoholic. There are so many knowing alcoholics out there, but they just don't want to change. There are ones that say "yeah, one more drink and then I'll change my life," but of course one drink turns into five and they're back in the same rut. Addiction is a hard barrier to overcome and we as humans need to realize that, in order to change anything in our lives, we need to want to change.

Being positive and following your goals to the end is hard. I know this. Escaping the rut that you're in and making the decision to change denote major obstacles. I know what it's like, and that first utterance that you want to change can be the hardest to state, but by changing your life and by building a happier and more positive mindset, you'll be able to build onto your life and create a wonderful, meaningful example for yourself.

Change is essentially that key propulsion that you need to achieve a more successful existence.

If you never fully decide to change, you're never going to be able to do what you'd like to change. You can sit here and read self-help books until the cows come home, or even just put lists upon lists together, but in order for this to work it must be a real change. I know people want to better their lives. Humans naturally desire to do so, and the biggest realization is that you're the one who starts the process of changing. It is you who brings it forward, and the one who in essence, transfers the idea to reality.

It isn't always the easiest thing to realize. After all, we are all humans, we tend to fall into the trap of our own ways,

but the truth is, if you change your thoughts, you can stop yourself from falling into this abyss even further.

What can you do, though? Well, I've highlighted below what you should consider and specific aspects to help you really enjoy success in terms of your thinking.

TIME TO THINK AND WRITE

To begin, you need to sit down and write down what you
want to change.

How to Change Your Thoughts

Be honest with yourself. Jot down what you feel will bring you the greatest benefits.

From there, look deeply at your thoughts. Be honest about what you're thinking about and your mindset regarding this part of life.

If it's positive, think about how you can reinforce that mindset. We will discuss positive thinking the next chapter.

If they are negative, actually look at the negative thoughts that you think when you contemplate them, and write them down. Critically analyse each of these negative thoughts and look at each in a realistic manner.

Once you see this trend, look at them and see why you believe them to be the case. What is the reasoning behind all of this negative thinking? Why do you feel that you won't reach your goals, and where does this negativity come from?? Try to pinpoint the origin of where those thoughts derived. If that person is still in your life, start to figure out a plan to not be as stifled by these impressions.

At this point, you'll want to rearrange your thoughts. Write down the positive thoughts that will align with your goals.

If you find yourself getting distracted, pull yourself back, and really focus on your thoughts to get back on track.

Once you've got your thoughts all in order, your next step is to start thinking about how you can apply this thought. Can you write it down, meditate on it each day, or cultivate something similar? Whatever the case may be, do this step, and put it together.

At this point, look at any additional factors that might be holding you back, whether they are in your head or otherwise. Think about ways you can protect yourself against negative thoughts, along with how you can improve at realizing when you're thinking negatively.

When it comes to enriching your life, you need to realize that you're going to hit those bumps in the road. They don't go away. The negative thoughts can be shut off and cast away, but they do sometimes come back, especially when you least expect them. You have to realize that life is a journey, for sure, but it is a journey worth pursuing. This mindset is especially true if you want to better your life and be more positive.

You need to understand that this step might take a little bit of time. After all you're looking at your goals, understanding what thoughts aren't aligned with them, and changing them. Positive thinking does play a big part in this key, and you also need to realize that you aren't perfect. You'll have your off days, but if you continue to work towards your goals, you're going to achieve your dreams.

Your thought process plays a huge part in the future you expedite. After all, if you do not really believe in yourself and are stuck in a negative rut, then you won't reach your goals. Negative thoughts will plague you in the worst way if you can't control them.

One thing to realize is that you may fall on your face, stumble a little bit, and struggle; however, if you do change your thoughts, you'll propel yourself into the right direction. Keep your thoughts in order and your goals will fall into place with success placed right on your lap as a result.

KEY 4:
CHANGING YOUR MINDSET
TO POSITIVE THINKING

Now that you recognize that your mindset plays a critical role in how you're able to change your life, it's time to learn about another key part of this process: you're your thinking.

Positive thinking is very powerful. It can change your life, and it can exemplify a huge step in the right direction. It can help you to bring everything together, and it can alter your attitude in life.

It's magical how much positive thinking can change you. You may realize over time that even just changing a small aspect of your mindset can make you better than ever! It can make those scary moments seem not as scary, that's for sure.

If you're looking to get better at positive thinking, you should consider changing your mindset

It is easier said than done though, but even just being a little bit more positive can change you. Have you ever witnessed TV shows or movies where the hero knows that death is near, that the bad guy is about to kill him, but he's got the mindset that he can win? He thinks he can save everyone, and then manages to do so usually. While fiction may exaggerate this correlation quite a bit, it's still applicable to your life. You should understand how to change the different aspects of your life with a little bit of positive thinking. Shifting your mindset to that of positivity can help you overcome troublesome situations. The unfortunate truth of it is that it's very easy to fall into a negative mindset. After all, it's like a bug, eating away at you if you're not careful. But, if you can keep a positive mindset, then you will win. In essence, if you're able to truly master the art of positivity, you'll be able to make anything work!

Positivity Vs. "Rose Colored Glasses" Thinking

Now thinking positively isn't some fake "rose-colored glasses" type of thinking. Rose-colored glasses make us think about fantasies, when in truth you need to accept the reality of your situation.

Correct thinking works to acknowledge the reality, but also helps you keep a positive mindset. It is being realistic about the situation, but also not succumbing to the doom and gloom of negativity.

Sure, you can "believe in the best" but the truth is that type of thinking doesn't always take into account the realism necessary. Yes, miracles can happen, but you have to be realistic with your thoughts, and work towards a more positive life. Let's say you want a better job and want to escape retail hell. Rose-colored glasses thinking would be "I want to be the CEO of an investment company right away" which is almost impossible because usually people can't get there immediately, unless of course they have dumb luck or connections. Or, it could be thinking you'll have a couple million dollars just by doing one single investment.

Of course, it can happen, but it's not realistic. That's just going to create losses.

Now, how about you sit down and articulate, "I want to quit my retail job and start to work in investing. I want to make my first sale by ___.

I can become an investor" and from there, you work towards that goal. It's realistic to be an investor, but you're not going to just snap your fingers and become the next Warren Buffet. You have to keep a positive mindset, but also be realistic with your thinking.

So how do you switch to the right thoughts and keep the negative at bay? Well, I'm going to explain that, but let's take a moment to talk about where these negative thoughts originate.

The Source of Negative Thoughts

So what's the source of most negative thoughts? Well, there are a few typical sources, and they are listed below:

- Your past experiences

- Anticipation of bad things for the future

- Your own personal fears

- Your fear of not having control

You can typically take any negative thought and look at each of these reasons, and you'll find that they'll fit into one or more of these examples. Let's take each of these and go into more detail on how they fit into negative thoughts.

For past experiences, you can figure this one out easily. You could for example, have had the dream to be a doctor, but your parents kept putting you down for that, saying "you'll never do it" or "schooling is too expensive, you'll never make it" or "you have to be smart to be one of those." Even if the thought is innocuous in intent, so it's often detrimental to your goals. Negative experiences, whether they reflect a parent, an ex who treated you badly, or former "friends" who didn't want you to succeed, all can really do a number on your thinking.

Anticipation of the future plays a big part in your negative thoughts as well, too. If you anticipate bad things, you're going to get bad things.

A good way to see this in life is if you believe you won't get the job, you won't.

Even just being positive in "I have a strong feeling I'll get the job" can change the mindset, and help you achieve your dreams.

The future can be scary, but if you know how to face it, and realize that while it is variable, there is still a chance that you'll survive. Again, it can make a huge difference.

Fears are another issue. Fear is something we all have. Fearing if you might fail is something that's more common than you'd think. We don't want to fail. When we fail, it's like we are losing a little bit of our own survival and presence in this world. If you have fears, you're worried about failing, and your fears could make you obsess over failure.

What happens when you obsess? Well, if you obsess over failure, it'll be very hard to really think in a positive mindset, so all of those fears that you had beforehand will continue to linger there like a festered wound, and you're not going to be successful. If you learn how to face these trepidations, and not obsess over them so much, you'll realize that you won't feel as negative and it can create a more positive mindset.

Finally, there's the inability to control the outcome, which can cause negative thoughts. If there is something beyond your aspects of control, you're going to fear the results, and often, that can make you obsess over failure, and you'll go down the slippery slope of negativity. If you are unable to control something, it can wreak havoc on your own personal feelings. But, sometimes realizing that there are just some things that you can't completely control can help you to feel better, too.

These reasons do tend to overlap in some cases. I remember a few times where I was negative about something, and it was due to not just based on my personal fears and worries, but also because I honestly had no clue

what the future held for me. I was scared, and that caused the negative thoughts to seep out excessively. I wasn't in control of situations either, and let me tell you, it's so easy to slip into that. But, you have to realize that slipping into those negative thoughts won't do you any good.

Simply put, negativity doesn't do much good in any situation, if at all. You need to be positive, and not allow negative thoughts to ruin your life.

It's amazing and slightly terrifying what negative thoughts can do to you. Even just one little inkling of negativity can breed negative thoughts, and it can stop you from achieving what you truly want.

You need to think positivity, because the wheels of motion will turn in your direction. It's hard to embrace this power, but once you work on this and start to change your thought process, things will magically fall into place.

Just like the hero that knew he could beat the enemy, you can get that job, find a girlfriend, and really be successful, if you just turn on that switch! o

How to Turn the Switch On

How do you turn it on, though? Well, there are many ways to do so. Here are some tips to become successful.

First, start to look at every negative thought. Write it down, and from there, change it so it's a positive thought.

Take these positive thoughts and work to reinforce this type of thinking. You can put them on sticky notes, write them down, whatever. You should keep these at the front of your thoughts, and just have gentle reminders all over the place in different ways.

Every single day, look at these positive thoughts. Maybe hang them on your fridge, or your dashboard in your car. Write them at the top of your daily planner. Look at them and learn to remember these as frequently as you can.

If you catch yourself being negative, stop, think about why you are negative, and switch gears.

If you have a negative thought that has been lingering for a long time, sit down and look at the source of it. If it's something from childhood, start to look and see why you're letting it hinder you. Realistically look and assess if that person is in your life anymore or not. Whatever it might be, be real with yourself and work to make those external factors less detrimental.

Finally, if you see yourself slipping into the trap of negative thoughts, keep that positivity there.

Remember that with very single dream and goal that you're positive about, always look at it in a realistic sense, and not through rose-colored glasses.

Thinking positively is harder than you'd think. I know, even in the worst of situations it's hard to stay positive. But, the law of attraction plays a critical role here. If you're negative, you're going to breed negativity!

It's scary how accurate this premise is, but look at your own life. If you've ever felt like you're just not doing well, sometimes a small change in your thinking will give you a better focus and outlook on life.

Work on turning that switch on. Work on being more positive. Sure life isn't always sunshine and rainbows, but being a little bit more positive can go a long way.

Positivity plays a huge part in your successes, and it's a key you're going to have to work on and change, especially if you want good things in life.

KEY 5:
LEARNING TO ACCEPT
YOURSELF

Being yourself is something that can be hard to do, but also quite easy. Being yourself will allow you to actually see yourself for who you are, and it's a big part of positive thinking.

Why is that? Well, read on to learn why this notion is one of the seven keys to success.

Why Be Yourself?

Being yourself is something many preach, but few actually do. You see this idea on social media, where people will live fake lives Being yourself allows you to harness your true potential. Being the real you can skyrocket you to new heights, and allow you to really make it.

It is natural to be you. Anyone who meets you when you're the real you will understand you in a better sense. By being yourself, you will create a bond that can make your life even better. If you're honest, confessing your "sins" and showing your true self, people will understand you.

For those of us who are scared to do really be yourself it can hold us back tremendously. Being unable to trust others, to be ourselves around others, whether it was because of a past experience or even just your own distrust, can constrain you. If you're able to be yourself you'll create deeper friendships, and bonds that can change you.

It also can drastically help with negative energy, since many sources of negativity are from times when we really aren't ourselves.

By being yourself, you won't need to spend energy on negativity, and it will allow you to be freer. I you can accept your faults, and really see yourself for who you are, you can learn to create a more positive life.

At the end of the day, who do you end up seeing in the mirror? Yourself. Do you want to see a version of yourself that's happy, positive, successful, and overall just doing good? Or would you like to see someone who is lying to himself or herself in the mirror constantly?

It sucks seeing that fake mask every single day. If you continue to lie to yourself, it tends to grow out of control, and then over time, you're living the life of a lie. Whether

it involves utilizing a persona that you think it healthy when in reality it's not, or even just trying to act like someone else for cheap likes and fake praise, you'll eventually realize that lying doesn't solve anything. Lying at the end of the day will make you feel terrible, unsuccessful and negative.

You need to as a person realize that lying never solves anything, and being yourself is the biggest tip that you can do to better yourself.

How Being yourself Connects to Positive Thinking

How does being yourself relate to positive thinking?

Well that's simple. If you're not trying to put on these false personas all the time, you'll realize that you have a lot more energy.

Have you ever seen a person go from a job that one abhors to a dream job? The change tends to make a person more energetic, positive, and you'll notice more successful vibes to this person. Being yourself, taking off the mask and seeing yourself for who you are will give you that burst of energy that you can put towards your goals.

Lying to yourself and pretending to enjoy something that you ultimately hate, will inevitably ruin you. I can't tell you how many times I've seen people working a job that they hate, pretending to be something that they're not, and overall just filled with negativity.

It's magical, and you'll see the mask practically peel away over time if you learn to be yourself!

Positive thinking plays a major role in being yourself. Sometimes you do need to grin and bear it, to push yourself into positivity, and from there, you'll see changes. But if you're not living your own life you're going to be unhappy.

You will realize positive thinking is totally possible and almost seamless if you're being yourself. You won't be embroiled by those negative thoughts because you're not hiding the truth. It can make or break you in many cases, and if you're honest, it will ultimately empower you!

You'll also realize that you're more self-reliant. You don't have to rely on others, because you're being yourself, and if you can believe it, you can totally achieve it. It opens the channels of positive thinking and makes it even better for you. You won't need to edit your personality to really

make yourself look good, but you can start to be yourself, accept your imperfections, and heal from your past trauma

Remember, if you want to heal any issues you have with yourself, whatever they may be you need to be honest with yourself.

Tips to Being Yourself

Here are some tips to reach your true potential and be yourself:
First, realistically look at how you are.
Is this persona truly yourself?
Or are you latching onto other people's personas?
If you answer the latter, what are you latching onto in life?
Why are you doing this false facade? I
s there a loss involved?
If there is one, ask yourself why you can't move on,
what is holding you back?
Work to pull yourself from that point in the past.
If you have a problem going on, look at the thoughts that are there.
Are they negative?
Are you truly being yourself?

Be honest, and look at every thought that you have!

If you don't feel like you're being yourself, analyze, and understand what being yourself is. If needed, you will want to learn how to filter your thoughts, and if you notice a thought that really isn't yours, you will realize it, and be able to switch it.

Meditation can help significantly. Take a thought, really think of one that pertains to being yourself, and meditate on it. If you feel intruding or negative thoughts rearing their ugly head, you can switch these calmly. Switch them, don't fight them, because it will prevent them from materializing.

Finally, work to part with the past. If you assumed a persona because of issues in the past, learn to part with it. Learn to accept that it was a part of your past, and you don't need to focus on it anymore.

How to Put These Factors Together

There are a few ways to merge these tips together, and I want to touch upon them here.

What you need to do first and foremost, is look at what is holding you back from being yourself. In my opinion, that's the first thing, and it also ties into measuring your success and worth. At this point, I think it's safe to say that if you want to be positive, and be successful, you need to stop pretending to be something you're not. Stop the negative thoughts, stop trying to compare yourself to others, and from here, work on positivity.

When you are finally yourself, you'll realize that it's quite easy to be positive. Sure, life isn't always sunshine and rainbows, but the reality of it is simpler and more fun. You'll just feel better, and you'll be happier.

You should also be yourself in measurement to your own success. If you do that, you'll be able to from here, create the life that you want to, and the mindset that fits with who you truly are.

So yes, if you're not being yourself, you're going to have a rough time, and you're going to realize as well that it does affect your ultimate success, both in life and in the future.

Being yourself plays a critical role in your ability to be successful, so it's very important that, if you aren't being true to yourself, you start to be true to yourself in whatever ways possible.

KEY 6:
REALIZING MISTAKES ARE JUST A SIMULATOR TO MAKE YOU STRONGER

Mistakes. They're something that we all make, and something that can be quite frustrating. Problems typically are a huge part of this process, too. How can we overcome these blunders? What are some great ways to fix these glitches, in order to help facilitate positive thinking and to live a better life? Well, read on to discover the truths!

Problems Are New Perspectives

That's the truth of it. Problems are new perspectives that you can look at and participating in resolving.

For example, let's say you have an issue at your job and you're worried about solving it. Accept it as a new perspective and look at different ways to really solve it. These tactics will help you to better understand and bring forth new ideas.

One thing you must stop yourself from doing is thinking that problems are the end-all, and that problems are always negative. Problems are not generally always bad. They happen. Apply this premise.

You literally can't avoid problems. There will always be a problem, whether significant or otherwise, and you need to, as a person, realize that these problems are perspectives that you must use to look forward, and determine for the possible outcomes yourself.

If you do look at problems in this way, I can guarantee that they will be easier to face, and you'll be able to face your problems with a new outlook that's genuinely better for you, and a healthier mindset than otherwise.

You can't just zap a problem and make it magically go away (although I wish you could), but by looking at this through that perspective, it can make it a little easier on everyone.

Remember, new perspectives are always there. Problems aren't the end of everything. Try to look at problems with the idea that you can learn something from them.

After all, they are learning experiences that allow you to change your thinking!

Mistakes Are Like a Simulator

Mistakes will happen. Problems will occur. These realities are all parts of life, and you need to realize, that in order to live a successful life with positive thinking, you must understand mistakes are bound to happen, problems are inescapable, and mistakes are essentially simulators. Even if they're big mistakes, they're not the end of the world if they happen.

If something does come up, you learn from it, so that next time, you don't do the same thing! Treating mistakes as simulations, even big mistakes, can help you immensely. We tend to hyper focus on mistakes to the point where we think it's the end of the world.

But that mindset breeds negativity, and that's how you get into negative mindsets.

So yes, realize that you can make mistakes and you WILL make mistakes at some point in your life.

But treating them as simulator that you can learn from will make you stronger and help you to vastly improve!

Mistakes can essentially serve as a means for assessing a different result from your actions. Let us take, for example, that you decide to work on a project. You choose to wait until the last minute, and then you're scrambling. You make mistakes, and you may be unhappy with the outcome. But let's take a look at it through a different mindset.

This time around you see that mistake as a simulator for what could happen in the future. Maybe you don't want to make that again, so you know what you do. You stop making that mistake.

You don't wait till the last second to get something to another person, you don't wait until the clock strikes midnight to do something, you work on yourself, and by putting it together, and realizing that this is a simulation for what not to do, you'll feel better.

Remember, you don't even need to dwell on these disappointments. Treating them as such will make them insignificant in your life, and in turn will help with breeding a more positive experience as a result of it all.

Learning to Part with the Past

If you want to have a new life or anything new, you've got to say goodbye to the past. The past is the past, and if you spend a ton of time thinking about it, you're sitting there breeding negativity and it won't make you stronger.

If you are hurt by someone, you'll immediately think about it, and from there, you'll think you've offended him or her. That obsession with feeling offended and affronted will eat

away at you like a festering wound, and that's how you get in trouble. Learning to let go of the past, even with people who were awful to you, can make a world of a difference.

So how do you do that? Well, you need to learn first of all to forgive, and from there understand that the person is working on their own lives, and you shouldn't worry about trying to teach them lessons. Instead, you need to just let it go.

Forgiving can be hard. But, if you sit down, look at various people who have offended and hurt you, and realistically look to see if you're not over it. From there, you want to look at how you can forgive this person and how you can get it out of your head.

Take those thoughts and learn to forgive. Put them in the right order within your head. Learn to unload them to somewhere where you can just go "that's in the past. I don't have to worry about it." Clearing out the negativity will allow you to do something else with them and make room for something better.

The past is always going to be there. Unfortunately, you can't fully escape your past. It will be there, and your choice of looking at it, obsessing over it or letting it affect you is up to you. You can let that happen, or you can let this just go its merry way and be much happier as a result.

The past will always be there, and you can choose whether you let it control you, or you control it! Plus, sometimes your past may play a part in how you generate success.

If you're basing your worth on something unsavory someone told you in the past, or even just on a mistake, you're going to feel unhappy and you're going to be negative. It is better if you learn not to worry so much about what happened in the past, and learn how to do it better next time. Remember that "the first to forgive is typically the strongest" so if you want to come out on top, and happier than before, you need to learn forgiveness, especially if you're trying to release yourself from the confines of negative thoughts.

People will hurt you. Unfortunately, the past can eat away at you, and it's awful to deal with at times. You should start to look at life with the outlook of forgiving and letting it go, because it is healthier, and it can change you.

Recalling Pleasant Memories

Finally, learn to recall pleasant memories. Instead of obsessing over the past and any negativity, you should learn to recall memories that are pleasant for you to really cherish. You should, whenever you feel like those negative thoughts are invading, sit down and recall something that's happy and pleasant.

You can think about maybe a good meal you had, your first kiss, whatever it might be. This recollection can take you out of the negative thoughts.

Pleasant memories make a difference. Sometimes, if you're too negative and need a pick-me-up, recalling a pleasant memory will allow you to bring forth a new idea, and you'll feel better about yourself. Even just remembering something small can bring your spirits up, and it's something I love doing when I know the going is getting tough and I just need to figure out for myself how to feel better. It is better to sit back, remember a good experience, and experience that positive energy again. It can help lift you up from the mud of negativity, and even just doing this tactic for a few minutes a day will change you. Once that's done, go back to the present. Look at what you're trying to solve. If it's a mistake, don't worry so much. If it's a problem, remember there are different perspectives. From there, you can work on it, and you can work towards your goals. Breed that positivity, since it can help you immensely.

This chapter showcased how you can learn to treat problems and the past in a better manner, and learn to let them go. It makes a world of a difference, and if you truly want to be happy, these tips offer the ultimate way to do it.

KEY 7:
THE POWER OF LOVE AND GRATITUDE

Love and gratitude play a major role in being happy and successful. Why is that? Well, remember that both of these are positive emotions. If you flood your life with positivity, you'll be much happier. Love will change your life, and the power of love will make you feel even better.

Psychologists have been studying this for years, and it's been seen that gratitude of all kinds, not just to spouses and partners, plays a major role in the happiness of others. This can create a cycle that's positive, and it will in turn improve the gratitude towards others.

So what is gratitude? How can you practice this and learning to love others? Read on to find out!

Gratitude is one of the simplest ways to really feel happier. If you're feeling down in the dumps, even just thinking "Well, I'm alive and happy, I can make others happy" will help you feel to better, and it is powerful.

Love, gratitude, and expressing positive emotions does seep into other parts of life, and it does help if you feel like there is a little bit of negativity and self-doubt brewing.

Love allows you to abandon a positive emotion. It doesn't have to be lovey-dovey romantic love, but friend love, platonic love, love for a pet, whatever it might be, can help you to stay grounded and have a more positive mindset. Every time you need some positive energy, just think about love. Love is powerful. Love is something that allows you to truly be successful.

How to Embrace the Power of Love

How can you embrace this without going immediately to romantic love, or the idea that you don't have a partner? Well first, write down all of the different aspects of life that make you feel really happy, such as maybe a cat, dog, a best friend, or even a parent that you can talk to honestly.

Look at this person and from there, write down how you can express love and embrace it.

From there, actually do it. If you have a cat, maybe even just sitting near it and petting it, and saying you love them can help.

If you have a partner, really tell them that you love them, and tell them you're thankful for them. Nice gestures they'll enjoy, such as cooking their favourite meal, or even cuddling, and watching their favourite movie can help.

For family, spending time with them and really talking to them, not just out of pure obligation, can help you to better embrace the power of love.

The same rule goes for friends. Spend time with them. Look to make sure you're really giving them the experience that they can enjoy. It is worth it to show your friends that you love them. Even if it's just telling them that, they'll appreciate it, and it will make them feel god.

This approach breeds a whole lot of positive energy. It's so simple!

Plus, if you really do feel like you're being overwhelmed by negativity, it is one of the best and most sure fire ways to make sure that you're giving yourself a life that you feel you can really make, and a life that you desire.

Love plays a major role in being positive and generating positive thinking. Learn to love more, for it can help you feel better and give you a chance to live a better life! As Lao Tzu said "being loved by somebody gives you strength, but learning to love someone is how you learn courage" and if you want to be stronger than before, this is something worth learning.

How to Express Gratitude

Gratitude is a great way to also express love. After all, being told that you're thankful for someone is a powerful tool to enable energy to resonate within you. So, how can you express gratitude better? Well, here are some cool ways to do so. First, you should write down everything that you're thankful for within your life. Literally just take everything that you're thankful for and write it down concisely. Research says that if you practice gratitude, you'll start to let go of toxic emotions. For example, Robert Emmons, in a study that he did as a gratitude researcher, found out from many studies that there is a link between well-bring and the practice of gratitude, and his research confirmed that if you practice gratitude, you can increase happiness, reduce depression, and you can let go of toxic emotions including resentment and envy.

From there, think about how you can express gratitude. If it's a partner, you can tell him or her this appreciation, or even just give them or do something for them. You can choose what to do.

At this point, you can from there, start to express gratitude towards others. Learn to be more humble, and start to be thankful for what others do.

Another great thing to do is more of a meditative exercise. When you wake up in the morning, say to yourself what you're thankful for. Be honest about it, and really see what you're thankful for. It doesn't have to be much, just a few things will do.

If you really do focus on this technique, and target the good rather than the bad, you'll be able to create a better, more rewarding experience possible.

Sometimes, a simple way to express gratitude is to just go out and observe people. Become more mindful of the world around you. Look around at the sights and one fun thing I enjoy is looking at the beauty of life and figuring out a couple of things I appreciate from the sight.

Even if it's something as simple as "The grass looks greener," will play a major role in the way I look at life. A little bit of observation can make you feel better, and it does make you appreciate life and the little nuances!

One of the keys to positive thinking is expressing love and gratitude, due to the fact that both of these are indeed positive emotions that you can express towards others. If you're not doing either of these rituals, it may be in your best interests to do so since it will allow for you to live a happier, more fulfilling life.

In turn, you can work on being a more positive person as a result of this.

Positive thinking doesn't have to be hard; you just need to focus on each of these points and work to express love and gratitude that you'll be able to show to others.

CONCLUSION

From this book, you've learned the importance of creating a positive life and why these seven keys are able to foster the mindset that you desire, and the life you wish to achieve. For many, having a positive life can really make a difference in many ways.

All of these concepts build upon one another. If you're wondering if your personal image plays a part in even expressing gratitude and accepting you may make mistakes, the answer is yes, it does. If you learn to harness each of these keys, you'll be on the road to true happiness. Do you feel like you're not reaching your true potential in life? Do you feel like you're not doing as well as your friends and peers? These seven keys can help you to clearly focus and independently create the experience that you desire. In turn, you'll be able to see the eminent difference. It doesn't take long to see results. All too often, if you change your mindset almost immediately, a difference will be seen.

People will react to you better, you'll be happier, and you'll notice almost immediately that your dreams will come true. It's amazing just what it can do for you, and the different potential that's out there. You'll be able to from here, create a life full of positivity, and you'll see just what kind of a difference it will make in time.

So don't fear the changes. Don't see the mistakes as a reason for giving up. Don't hold onto the regrets from the past, or obsess over people who wronged you. These practices are not the key to happiness, but are often the key to feeling the negativity boiling within you. Instead of negative feelings, start to create a positive life, and work towards that happiness for yourself, and for others as well.

Remember that Willie Nelson said, "Once you replace negative thoughts with positive ones, you'll start having positive results," and that's something that everyone can achieve. Replacing this is the first step to success, and you can better your life in many different ways with just a few simple changes.

Made in the USA
San Bernardino, CA
22 July 2020